Rhyme Time
A B C

an alphabet adventure from
A to Z

written & illustrated by
May Killebrew Hanna

Copyright © 2023 by May Killebrew Hanna

All rights reserved. No part of this publication may be reproduced, stored, or transmitted in any form or by any means, electronic, mechanical, photocopying, recording, scanning, or otherwise, without written permission from the publisher. It is illegal to copy this book, post it to a website, or distribute it by any other means without permission.

May Killebrew Hanna asserts the moral right to be identified as the author of this work.

First edition

For Elli

A

is for Airplane high in the sky,

a is for alligator swimming by.

B
is for Butterfly flitting around,

b

is for banana yellow and round.

C is for Cat cuddly and cute,

C is for car tooting its hoot.

D is for Duck swimming along,

E

is for
Elephant
giant
and
gray,

e

is for eggs in the nest where they lay.

F

is for Fish swimming at sea,

f is for fox running wild and free.

G

is for Giraffe
with neck
so long,

g

is for grape in a bunch, so strong.

H is for Horse prancing with glee,

h is for hive the home of the bee.

I is for Inchworm having some fun,

i is for iguana lying in the sun.

J is for jungle, with monkeys that swing,

j is for juice, that makes your mouth zing.

K

is for King
so regal
and grand,

k is for koala such cute tiny hands.

L is for Lion with a mighty roar,

l is for ladybug
with spots, galore.

M is for Mushroom growing in the ground,

N is for Night when the stars shine bright,

n
is for noodles such a tasty delight!

O is for Ocean so vast and so blue,

O
is for Octopus with 4 arms times 2!

P is for Pig rolling in mud,

p is for panda so cute and so snug.

Q is for Quiet when we need to hear,

q is for quick like a small bouncing deer.

R is for Rocket zooming through the sky,

r is for robot, with one flashing eye.

S is for snail with his slow, slimy tread.

T

is for Tree tall and green,

t is for tiger fierce and keen.

U

is for Umbrella to keep you dry,

U

is for unicorn
up in the sky.

V is for Volcano hot and loud,

V is for violin playing proud.

W is for Water, that we drink each day,

W is for weasel who loves to play.

X

is for xylophone with keys that we tweak

Y is for Yellow like the shining sun,

y is for yummy! a treat for everyone.

Z is for Zebra with stripes so nice,

Z

is for Zamboni smoothing the ice.

Congratulations!

You've made it to the end.
You've learned your ABC's
my little friend.

From A to Z, you've come so far,
Now it's time to share,
how smart you are!